OEDIPUS REX
(OEDIPUS THE KING)

By Sophocles

Translated by E. H. Plumptre

D1167248

A Digireads.com Book
Digireads.com Publishing
16212 Riggs Rd
Stilwell, KS, 66085

Oedipus Rex (Oedipus the King)
By Sophocles
Translated by E. H. Plumptre
ISBN: 1-4209-2603-9

Introductory Note

SOPHOCLES, the most perfectly balanced among the three great masters of Greek tragedy, was born in Colonus, near Athens, about 495 B. C. His father was a man of wealth, and the poet received the best education of the time, being especially distinguished in music. He began his career as a dramatist at the age of twenty-seven, when he gained a victory over Æschylus; and from that time till his death in 405 B. C. he retained the foremost place as a writer of tragedy. Like a true Greek, he played his part in public affairs, both in peace and in war, and served his country as a diplomat and as a general. He was profoundly admired by his contemporaries for character as well as genius, and after his death was honored as a hero with annual sacrifices. His son, Iophon, and his grandson, Sophocles, both gained distinction as tragic poets.

Besides lyrics, elegies, and epigrams, Sophocles is said to have composed upward of one hundred and twenty plays, one hundred of which are known by name, but only seven have come down to us entire. These are the "Trachiniæ," dealing with the death of Heracles; "Ajax," "Philoctetes," "Electra," "Oedipus Rex," "Oedipus at Colonus," and "Antigone."

The development of tragedy by Æschylus was continued by Sophocles, who introduced a third actor and, later, a fourth; reduced still further the importance of the chorus, and elaborated the costumes of the players. He did not, like Æschylus, write trilogies which carried one story through three plays, but made each work complete in itself. The art of clear and full characterization was carried to a pitch of perfection by him, the figures in the plays of Æschylus being in comparison rather drawings in outline, while those of Euripides are frequently direct transcripts from real life, without the idealization given by Sophocles. With his restraint, his balance, his clearness of vision, his aptness in the fitting of means to ends, and the beauty of his style, he stands as the most perfect example in literature of the characteristic excellences of the Greek artist. In the two dramas here given will be found illustrations of these qualities at their highest.

Dramatis Personæ

Oedipus, King of Thebes
Creon, brother of Jocasta
Teiresias, a soothsayer
Priest of Zeus
Messenger from Corinth
Shepherd
Second Messenger
Jocasta, wife of Oedipus
Chorus of Priests and Suppliants

SCENE—Thebes. In the background, the palace of
OEDIPUS; in front, the altar of ZEUS, Priests and Boys
round it in the attitude of suppliants.

[*Enter* OEDIPUS]

OEDIPUS.

    WHY sit ye here, my children, brood last reared
    Of Cadmus famed of old, in solemn state,
    Uplifting in your hands the suppliants' boughs?
    And all the city reeks with incense smoke,
    And all re-echoes with your wailing hymns;
    And I, my children, counting it unmeet
    To hear report from others, I have come
    Myself, whom all name Oedipus the Great.—
    Do thou, then, agèd Sire, since thine the right
    To speak for these, tell clearly why ye stand
    Awe-stricken, or adoring; speak to me
    As willing helper. Dull and cold this heart
    To see you prostrate thus, and feel no ruth.

PRIEST.

    Yes, Oedipus, thou ruler of my land,
    Thou seest us how we sit, as suppliants, bowed
    Around thine altars; some as yet unfledged
    To wing their flight, and some weighed down with age.
    Priest, I, of Zeus, and these the chosen youth:
    And in the open spaces of the town
    The people sit and wail, with wreath in hand,
    By the twin shrine of Pallas, or the grove
    Oracular that bears Ismenus' name.
    For this our city, as thine eyes may see,
    Is sorely tempest-tossed, nor lifts its head
    From out the surging sea of blood-flecked waves,
    All smitten in the fruitful blooms of earth,
    All smitten in the herds that graze the fields,
    Yea, and in timeless births of woman's fruit;
    And still the God sends forth his darts of fire,

And lays us low. The plague, abhorred and feared,
Makes desolate the home where Cadmus dwelt,
And Hades dark grows rich in sighs and groans.
It is not that we count thee as a God,
Equalled with them in power, that we sit here,
These little ones and I, as suppliants prone;
But, judging thee, in all life's shifting scenes,
Chiefest of men, yea, and of chiefest skill,
To soothe the powers of Heaven. For thou it was
That freed'st this city, named of Cadmus old,
From the sad tribute which of yore we paid
To that stern songstress, all untaught of us,
And all unprompted; but at God's behest,
Men think and say, thou guidest all our life.
And now, O Oedipus, most honoured lord,
We pray thee, we, thy suppliants, find for us
Some succour, whether floating voice of God,
Or speech of man brings knowledge to thy soul;
For still I see, with those whom life has trained
To long-tried skill, the issues of their thoughts
Live and are mighty. Come, then, noblest one,
Come, save our city; look on us, and fear.
As yet this land, for all thy former zeal,
Calls thee its saviour: do not give us cause
So to remember this thy reign, as men
Who, having risen, then fall low again;
But save us, save our city. Omens good
Were then with thee; thou didst thy work, and now
Be equal to thyself! If thou wilt rule,
As thou dost rule, this land wherein we dwell,
'Twere better far to reign o'er living men
Than o'er a realm dispeopled. Naught avails,
Or tower or ship, when crew and guards are gone.

OEDIP.

> O children, wailing loud, ye tell me not
> Of woes unknown; too well I know them all,
> Your sorrows and your wants. For one and all
> Are stricken, yet no sorrow like to mine
> Weighs on you. Each his own sad burden bears,
> His own and not another's. But my heart
> Mourns for the people's sorrow and mine own;
> And, lo! ye have not come to break my sleep,
> But found me weeping, weeping bitter tears,
> And treading weary paths in wandering thought;
> And that one way of healing which I found,
> That have I acted on. Menœkeus' son,
> Creon, my kinsman, have I sent to seek
> The Pythian home of Phœbus, there to learn
> The words or deeds wherewith to save the state;
> And even now I measure o'er the time
> And wonder how he fares, for, lo! he stays,
> I know not why, beyond the appointed day;
> But when he comes I should be base indeed,
> Failing to do whate'er the God declares.

PRIEST.

> Well hast thou spoken! Tidings come e'en now
> Of Creon seen approaching.

OEDIP.

> Grant, O King
> Apollo, that he come with omen good,
> Bright with the cheer of one that bringeth life.

PRIEST.
> If one may guess, 'tis well. He had not come
> His head all wreathed with boughs of laurel else.

OEDIP.
> Soon we shall know. Our voice can reach him now.
> Say, prince, our well-beloved, Menœkeus' son,
> What sacred answer bring'st thou from the God?

[Enter CREON]

CREON.
> A right good answer! That our evil plight,
> If all goes well, may end in highest good.

OEDIP.
> What means this speech? Nor full of eager hope,
> Nor trembling panic, list I to thy words.

CREON.
> I for my part am ready, these being by,
> To tell thee all, or go within the gates.

OEDIP.
> Speak out to all. I sorrow more for them
> Than for the woe which touches me alone.

CREON.
> Well, then, I speak the things the God declared.
> Phœbus, our king, he bids us chase away
> (The words were plain) the infection of our land,
> Nor cherish guilt which still remains unhealed.

OEDIP.
>But with what rites? And what the deed itself?

CREON.
>Drive into exile, blood for blood repay.
>That guilt of blood is blasting all the state.

OEDIP.
>But whose fate is it that thou hintest at?

CREON.
>Once, O my king, ere thou didst raise our state,
>Our sovereign Laius ruled o'er all the land.

OEDIP.
>This know I well, though him I never saw.

CREON.
>Well, then, the God commands us, he being dead,
>To take revenge on those who shed his blood.

OEDIP.
>Yes; but where are they? How to track the course
>Of guilt all shrouded in the doubtful past?

CREON.
>In this our land, so said he, those who seek
>Shall find; unsought, we lose it utterly.

OEDIP.
>Was it at home, or in the field, or else
>In some strange land that Laius met his doom?

CREON.

> He went, so spake he, pilgrim-wise afar,
> And nevermore came back as forth he went.

OEDIP.

> Was there no courier, none who shared his road,
> From whom, inquiring, one might learn the truth?

CREON.

> Dead are they all, save one who fled for fear,
> And he had naught to tell but this:...

OEDIP. [*interrupting*]

> And what was that? One fact might teach us much,
> Had we but one small starting-point of hope.

CREON.

> He used to tell that robbers fell on him,
> Not man for man, but with outnumbering force.

OEDIP.

> Yet sure no robber would have dared this deed,
> Unless some bribe had tempted him from hence.

CREON.

> So men might think; but Laius at his death
> Found none to help, or 'venge him in his woe.

OEDIP.

> What hindered you, when thus your sovereignty
> Had fallen low, from searching out the truth?

CREON.

> The Sphinx, with her dark riddle, bade us look
> At nearer facts, and leave the dim obscure.

OEDIP.

> Well, be it mine to track them to their source.
> Right well hath Phœbus, and right well hast thou,
> Shown for the dead your care, and ye shall find,
> As is most meet, in me a helper true,
> Aiding at once my country and the God.
> Not for the sake of friends, or near or far,
> But for mine own, will I dispel this curse;
> For he that slew him, whosoe'er he be,
> Will wish, perchance, with such a blow to smite
> Me also. Helping him, I help myself.
> And now, my children, rise with utmost speed
> From off these steps, and raise your suppliant boughs;
> And let another call my people here,
> The race of Cadmus, and make known that I
> Will do my taskwork to the uttermost:
> So, as God wills, we prosper, or we fail.

PRIEST.

> Rise, then, my children, 'twas for this we came,
> For these good tidings which those lips have brought,
> And Phœbus, he who sent these oracles,
> Pray that he come to heal, and save from woe.

[*Exeunt* CREON *and* Priest.]

STROPHE I

CHORUS.

    O voice of Zeus sweet-toned, with what intent
    Cam'st thou from Pytho, where the red gold shines,
    To Thebes, of high estate?
    Fainting for fear, I quiver in suspense
    (Hear us, O healer! God of Delos, hear!),
    In brooding dread, what doom, of present growth,
    Or as the months roll on, thy hand will work;
    Tell me, O Voice divine, thou child of golden hope!

ANTISTROPHE I

    Thee first, Zeus-born Athene, thee I call;
    And next thy sister, Goddess of our land,
    Our Artemis, who in the market sits
    In queenly pride, upon her orbed throne;
    And Phœbus, the fair darter! O ye Three,
    Shine on us, and deliver us from ill!
    If e'er before, when waves or storms of woe
        Rushed on our state, ye drove away
        The fiery tide of ill,
        Come also now!

STROPHE II

    Yea, come, ye Gods, for sorrows numberless
        Press on my soul;
    And all the host is smitten, and our thoughts
        Lack weapons to resist.
    For increase fails of all the fruits of earth,
    And women faint in childbirth's wailing pangs,
    And one by one, as flit the swift-winged birds,

So, flitting to the shore of Hades dark,
 Fleeter than lightning's flash,
 Thou seest them passing on.

ANTISTROPHE II

Yea, numberless are they who perish thus,
 And on the soil, plague-breeding, lie
Infants unpitied, cast out ruthlessly;
And wives and mothers, gray with hoary age,
Some here, some there, by every altar mourn,
 With woe and sorrow crushed,
 And chant their wailing plaint.
Clear thrills the sense their solemn litany,
And the low anthem sung in unison.
Hear, then, thou golden daughter of great Zeus,
And send us help, bright-faced as is the morn.

STROPHE III

And Ares the destroyer drive away!
Who now, though hushed the din of brazen shield,
With battle-cry wars on me fierce and hot.
 Bid him go back in flight,
 Retreat from this our land,
 Or to the ocean bed,
 Where Amphitrite sleeps,
 Or to the homeless sea
 Which sweeps the Thracian shore.
 If waning night spares aught
 That doth the day assail:
 Do thou, then, Sire almighty,
 Wielding the lightning's strength,
 Blast him with thy hot thunder.

ANTISTROPHE III

And thou, Lyceian king, the wolf's dread foe,
    Fain would I see thy darts
    From out thy golden bow
    Go forth invincible,
    Helping and bringing aid;
    And with them, winged with fire,
    The rays of Artemis,
    With which, on Lycian hills,
    She moveth on her course.
    And last I call on thee,
    Thou of the golden crown,
    Guardian of this our land,
    Bacchus, all purple-flushed,
    With clamour loud and long,
    Wandering with Maenads wild;
    I call on thee to come,
    Flashing with blazing torch,
Against the God whom all the Gods disown.

OEDIP.
    Thou prayest, and for thy prayers, if thou wilt hear
    My words, and treat the dire disease with skill,
    Thou shalt find help and respite from thy pain,—
    My words, which I, a stranger to report,
    A stranger to the deed, will now declare:
    For I myself should fail to track it far,
    Unless some footprints guided me aright.
    But now, since here I stand, the latest come,
    A citizen to citizens, I speak
    To all the sons of Cadmus. Lives there one
    Who knows of Laius, son of Labdacus,
    The hand that slew him; him I bid to tell
    His tale to me; and should it chance he shrinks,

Fearing the charge against himself to bring,
Still let him speak; no heavier doom is his
Than to depart uninjured from the land;
Or, if there be that knows an alien arm
As guilty, let him hold his peace no more;
I will secure his gain and thanks beside.
But if ye hold your peace, if one through fear
Shall stifle words his bosom friend may drop,
What then I purpose let him hear from me:
That man I banish, whosoe'er he be,
From out the land whose power and throne are mine;
And none may give him shelter, none speak to him,
Nor join with him in prayer and sacrifice,
Nor pour for him the stream that cleanses guilt;
But all shall thrust him from their homes, abhorred,
Our curse and our pollution, as the word
Prophetic of the Pythian God has shown:
Such as I am, I stand before you here,
A helper to the God and to the dead.
And for the man who did the guilty deed,
Whether alone he lurks, or leagued with more,
I pray that he may waste his life away,
For vile deeds vilely dying; and for me,
If in my house, I knowing it, he dwells,
May every curse I speak on my head fall.
And this I charge you do, for mine own sake,
And for the God's, and for the land that pines,
Barren and god-deserted. Wrong 'twould be,
E'en if no voice from heaven had urged us on,
That ye should leave the stain of guilt uncleansed,
Your noblest chief, your king himself, being slain.
Yea, rather, seek and find. And since I reign,
Wielding the might his hand did wield before,
Filling his couch, and calling his wife mine,
Yea, and our children too, but for the fate

That fell on his, had grown up owned by both;
But so it is. On his head fell the doom;
And therefore will I strive my best for him,
As for my father, and will go all lengths
To seek and find the murderer, him who slew
The son of Labdacus, and Polydore,
And earlier Cadmus, and Agenor old;
And for all those who hearken not, I pray
The Gods to give then neither fruit of earth,
Nor seed of woman, but consume their lives
With this dire plague, or evil worse than this.
And you, the rest, the men from Cadmus sprung,
To whom these words approve themselves as good,
May righteousness befriend you, and the Gods,
In full accord, dwell with you evermore.

CHORUS.

    Since thou hast bound me by a curse, O king,
    I needs must speak. I neither slew the man,
    Nor know who slew. To say who did the deed
    Belongs to him who sent this oracle.

OEDIP.

    Right well thou speak'st, but man's best strength must
      fail
    To force the Gods to do the things they will not.

CHORUS.

    And may I speak a second time my thoughts?

OEDIP.

    If 'twere a third, shrink not from speaking out.

CHORUS.

    One man I know, a prince, whose insight deep
    Sees clear as princely Phœbus, and from him,
    Teiresias, one might learn, O king, the truth.

OEDIP.

    That, too, is done. No loiterer I in this,
    For I have sent, on Creon's hint, two bands
    To summon him, and wonder that he comes not.

CHORUS.

    Old rumours are there also, dark and dumb.

OEDIP.

    And what are they? I weigh the slightest word.

CHORUS.

    'Twas said he died by some chance traveller's hand.

OEDIP.

    I, too, heard that. But none knows who was by.

CHORUS.

    If yet his soul is capable of awe,
    Hearing thy curses, he will shrink from them.

OEDIP.

    Words fright not him who, doing, knows no fear.

CHORUS.

    Well, here is one who'll put him to the proof.
    For, lo! they bring the seer inspired of God;
    Chosen of all men, vessel of the truth.

[Enter TEIRESIAS, *blind, and guided by a boy]*

OEDIP.

> Teiresias! thou whose mind embraceth all,
> Told or untold, the things of heaven or earth;
> Thou knowest, although thou seest not, what a pest
> Dwells on us, and we find in thee, O prince,
> Our one deliverer, yea, our only help.
> For Phœbus (if, perchance, thou hast not heard)
> Sent back this word to us, who sent to ask,
> That this one way was open to escape
> From the fell plague; if those who Laius slew,
> We in our turn, discovering, should slay,
> Or drive them forth as exiles from the land.
> Thou, therefore, grudge not either sign from birds,
> Or any other path of prophecy;
> But save the city, save thyself, save me;
> Lift off the guilt that death has left behind;
> On thee we hang. To use our means, our power,
> In doing good, is noblest service owned.

TEIR.

> Ah me! ah me! how sad is wisdom's gift,
> When no good issue waiteth on the wise!
> Right well I knew this, but in evil hour
> Forgot, alas! or else I had not come.

OEDIP.

> What means this? How despondingly thou com'st!

TEIR.

> Let me go home; for thus thy fate shalt thou,
> And I mine own, bear easiest, if thou yield.

OEDIP.

No loyal words thou speak'st, nor true to Thebes
Who reared thee, holding back this oracle.

TEIR.

It is because I see thy lips speak words
Ill-timed, ill-omened, that I guard my speech.

OEDIP.

Now, by the Gods, unless thy reason fails,
Refuse us not, who all implore thy help.

TEIR.

Yes. Reason fails you all; but ne'er will I
So speak my sorrows as to unveil thine.

OEDIP.

What mean'st thou, then? Thou know'st and wilt not
    tell,
But giv'st to ruin both the state and us?

TEIR.

I will not pain myself nor thee. Why, then,
All vainly urge it? Thou shalt never know.

OEDIP.

Oh, basest of the base! (for thou wouldst stir
A heart of stone;) and wilt thou never tell,
But still abide relentless and unmoved?

TEIR.

My mood thou blamest, but thou dost not know
That which dwells with thee while thou chidest me.

OEDIP.

    And who would not feel anger, as he hears
    The words which bring dishonour to the state?

TEIR.

    Well! come they will, though I should hold my peace.

OEDIP.

    If come they must, thy duty is to speak.

TEIR.

    I speak no more. So, if thou wilt, rage on,
    With every mood of wrath most desperate.

OEDIP.

    Yes; I will not refrain, so fierce my wrath,
    From speaking all my thought. I think that thou
    Didst plot the deed, and do it, though the blow
    Thy hands, it may be, dealt not. Hadst thou seen,
    I would have said it was thy deed alone.

TEIR.

    And it has come to this? I charge thee, hold
    To thy late edict, and from this day forth
    Speak not to me, nor yet to these, for thou,
    Thou art the accursèd plague-spot of the land.

OEDIP.

    Art thou so shameless as to vent such words,
    And thinkest to escape thy righteous doom?

TEIR.

    I have escaped. The strength of truth is mine.

OEDIP.

Who prompted thee? This comes not from thine art.

TEIR.

Thou art the man. 'Twas thou who mad'st me speak.

OEDIP.

What say'st thou? Tell it yet again, that I
May know more clearly.

TEIR.

When I spoke before,
Didst thou not know? Or dost thou challenge me?

OEDIP.

I could not say I knew it. Speak again.

TEIR.

I say that thou stand'st there a murderer.

OEDIP.

Thou shalt not twice revile, and go unharmed.

TEIR.

And shall I tell thee more to stir thy rage?

OEDIP.

Say what thou pleasest. All in vain 'tis said.

TEIR.

I say that thou, in vilest intercourse
With those thou lovest best, dost blindly live,
Nor seest the evil thou hast made thine own.

OEDIP.
> And dost thou think to say these things and live?

TEIR.
> Of that I doubt not, if truth holds her own.

OEDIP.
> Truth is for all but thee, but thou hast none,
> Blind in thine ears, thy reason, and thine eyes.

TEIR.
> How wretched thou, thus hurling this reproach!
> Such, all too soon, the world will hurl at thee.

OEDIP.
> Thou livest wrapt in one continual night,
> And canst not hurt or me, or any man
> Who sees the light.

TEIR.
> Fate's firm decree stands fixed:
> Thou diest not by me. Apollo's might
> Suffices. His the task to bring thee low.

OEDIP.
> Are these devices Creon's or thine own?

TEIR.
> It is not Creon harms thee, but thyself.

OEDIP.
> O wealth, and sovereignty, and noblest skill
> Surpassing skill in life that men admire,
> How great the envy dogging all your steps!
> If for the sake of kingship, which the state

Hath given, unasked for, freely in mine hands,
Creon the faithful, found mine earliest friend,
Now seeks with masked attack to drive me forth,
And hires this wizard, plotter of foul schemes,
A vagrant mountebank, whose sight is clear
For pay alone, but in his art stone-blind.
Is it not so? When wast thou known a seer?
Why, when the monster with her song was here,
Didst thou not give our countrymen thy help?
And yet the riddle lay above the ken
Of common men, and called for prophet's skill.
And this thou show'dst thou hadst not, nor by bird,
Nor any God made known; but then I came,
I, Oedipus, who nothing knew, and slew her,
With mine own counsel winning, all untaught
By flight of birds. And now thou wouldst expel me,
And think'st to take thy stand by Creon's throne.
But, as I think, both thou and he that plans
With thee, will to your cost attack my fame;
And but that thou stand'st there all old and weak,
Thou shouldst be taught what kind of plans are thine.

CHORUS.

Far as we dare to measure, both his words
And thine, O Oedipus, in wrath are said.
Not such as these we need, but this to see,
How best to do the bidding of the God.

TEIR.

King though thou be, I claim an equal right
To make reply. Here I call no man lord:
For I am not thy slave, but Loxias'.
Nor shall I stand on Creon's patronage;
And this I say, since thou hast dared revile
My blindness, that thou seest, yet dost not see

Thy evil plight, nor where thou liv'st, nor yet
With whom thou dwellest, Know'st thou even this,
Whence thou art sprung? All ignorant thou sinn'st
Against thine own, the living and the dead.
And soon a curse from mother and from sire
With fearful foot shall chase thee forth from us,
Now seeing all things clear, then all things dark.
And will not then each shore repeat thy wail,
And will not old Kithæron echoing ring
When thou discern'st the marriage, fatal port,
To which thy prosp'rous voyage brought thy bark?
And other ills, in countless multitude,
Thou seest not yet, on thee and on thy seed
Shall fall alike. Vent forth thy wrath then loud,
On Creon and on me. There lives not man
Who wastes his life more wretchedly than thou.

OEDIP.

This can be borne no longer! Out with thee!
A curse light on thee! Wilt thou not depart?
Wilt thou not turn and wend thy backward way?

TEIR.

I had not come hadst thou not called me here.

OEDIP.

I knew not thou wouldst speak so foolishly;
Else I had hardly fetched thee to my house.

TEIR.

We then, for thee (so deemest thou), are fools,
But, for thy parents, who begot thee, wise.
[*Turns to go.*]

OEDIP. [*starting forward*]
What? Stay thy foot. What mortal gave me birth?

TEIR.
This day shall give thy birth, and work thy doom.

OEDIP.
What riddles dark and dim thou lov'st to speak.

TEIR.
Yes. But thy skill excels in solving such.

OEDIP.
Scoff as thou wilt, in this thou'lt find me strong.

TEIR.
And yet success in this has worked thy fall.

OEDIP.
I little care, if I have saved the state.

TEIR.
Well, then, I go. Do thou, boy, lead me on!

OEDIP.
Let him lead on. So hateful art thou near,
Thou canst not pain me more when thou art gone.

TEIR.

I go, then, having said the things I came
To say. No fear of thee compels me. Thine
Is not the power to hurt me. And I say,
This man whom thou art seeking out with threats,
As murderer of Laius, he is here,
In show an alien sojourner, but in truth
A home-born Theban. No delight to him
Will that discovery bring. Blind, having seen,
Poor, having rolled in wealth,—he, with a staff
Feeling his way, to other lands shall go!
And by his sons shall he be known at once
Father and brother, and of her who bore him
Husband and son, sharing his father's bed,
His father's murd'rer. Go thou, then, within,
And brood o'er this, and, if thou find'st me fail,
Say that my skill in prophecy is gone.

[*Exeunt* OEDIPUS *and* TEIRESIAS.]

STROPHE I

CHORUS.

Who was it that the rock oracular
Of Delphi spake of, working
With bloody hand his nameless deed of shame?
Time is it now for him,
Swifter than fastest steed,
To bend his course in flight.
For, in full armour clad,
Upon him darts, with fire
And lightning flash, the radiant Son of Zeus.
And with him come in train the dreaded ones,
The Destinies that may not be appeased.

ANTISTROPHE I

For from Parnassus' heights, enwreathed with snow,
    Gleaming, but now there shone
The oracle that bade us, one and all,
    Track the unnamed, unknown one.
For, lo! he wanders through the forest wild,
    In caves and over rocks,
    As strays the mountain bull,
In dreary loneliness with dreary tread,
    Seeking in vain to shun
The words prophetic of the central shrine;
Yet they around him hover, full of life.

STROPHE II

Dread things, yea, dread, the augur skilled has stirred
That leave the question open, aye or no!
    And which to say I know not,
But hover still in hopes, and fail to scan
    Things present or to come.
For neither now nor in the former years
    Learnt I what cause of strife
    Set the Labdacid race
At variance with the house of Polybus.
    Nor can I test the tale,
And take my stand against the well-earned fame
    Of Oedipus, my lord,
As champion of the house of Labdacus,
    For deaths that none may trace!

ANTISTROPHE II

For Zeus and King Apollo, they are wise,
    And know the hearts of men:
But that a prophet passeth me in skill,
    This is no judgment true;
And one man may another's wisdom pass,
    By wisdom higher still.
I, for my part, before the word is clear,
Will ne'er assent to those that speak in blame.
'Tis clear, the Maiden-monster with her wings
Came on him, and he proved by sharpest test
That he was wise, by all the land beloved,
    And, from my heart at least,
    The charge of baseness comes not.

[*Enter* CREON]

CREON.
    I come, my friends, as having learnt but now
    Our ruler, Oedipus, accuses me
    With dreadful words I cannot bear to hear.
    For if, in these calamities of ours,
    He thinks he suffers wrongly at my hands,
    In word or deed, aught tending to his hurt,
    I set no value on a life prolonged,
    If this reproach hangs on me; for its harm
    Affects not slightly, but is direst shame,
    If through the land my name as villain rings,
    By thee and by thy friends a villain called.

CHORUS.

But this reproach, it may be, came from wrath
All hasty, rather than from judgment calm.

CREON.

And who informed him that the seer, seduced
By my false counsel, spoke his lying words?

CHORUS.

The words were said, but on what grounds I know not.

CREON.

And was it with calm eyes and judgment clear,
The charge was brought against my name and fame?

CHORUS.

I cannot say. To what our rulers do
I close my eyes. But here he comes himself.

[*Enter* OEDIPUS]

OEDIP.

Ho, there! is't thou? And does thy boldness soar
So shameless as to come beneath my roof,
When thou, 'tis clear, hast done the deed of blood,
And now wilt rob me of my sovereignty?
Is it, by all the Gods, that thou hast seen
Or cowardice or folly in my soul,
That thou hast laid thy plans? Or thoughtest thou
That I should neither see thy sinuous wiles,
Nor, knowing, ward them off? This scheme of thine,
Is it not wild, backed nor by force nor friends,
To seek the power which calls for force or wealth?

CREON.

> Do as thou pleasest. But for words of scorn
> Hear like words back, and as thou hearest, judge.

OEDIP.

> Cunning of speech art thou! But I am slow
> To learn of thee, whom I have found my foe.

CREON.

> Hear this, then, first, that thus I have to speak....

OEDIP.

> But this, then, say not, that thou art not vile.

CREON.

> If that thou thinkest self-willed pride avails,
> Apart from judgment, know thou art not wise.

OEDIP.

> If that thou thinkest, injuring thy friend,
> To do it unchastised, thou art not wise.

CREON.

> In this, I grant, thou speakest right; but tell,
> What form of suffering hast thou to endure?

OEDIP.

> Didst thou, or didst thou not, thy counsel give
> Some one to send to fetch this reverend seer?

CREON.

> And even now by that advice I hold!

OEDIP.

How long a time has passed since Laius chanced…
[*Pauses.*]

CREON.

Chanced to do what? I understand not yet.

OEDIP.

Since he was smitten with the deadly blow?

CREON.

The years would measure out a long, long tale.

OEDIP.

And was this seer then practising his art?

CREON.

Full wise as now, and equal in repute.

OEDIP.

Did he at that time say a word of me?

CREON.

No word, while I, at any rate, was by.

OEDIP.

And yet ye held your quest upon the dead?

CREON.

Of course we held it, but we nothing heard.

OEDIP.

How was it he, the wise one, spoke not then?

CREON.

I know not, and, not knowing, hold my peace.

OEDIP.

One thing thou know'st, and, meaning well, wouldst
speak!

CREON.

And what is that? for if I know, I'll speak.

OEDIP.

Why, unless thou wert in the secret, then
He spake not of me as the murderer.

CREON.

If he says this, thou know'st it. I of thee
Desire to learn, as thou hast learnt of me.

OEDIP.

Learn then; no guilt of blood shall rest on me.

CREON.

Well, then,—my sister? dost thou own her wife?

OEDIP.

I will not meet this question with denial.

CREON.

And sharest thou an equal rule with her?

OEDIP.

Her every wish by me is brought to act.

CREON.

And am not I co-equal with you twain?

OEDIP.

Yes; and just here thou show'st thyself false friend.

CREON.

Not so, if thou wouldst reason with thyself,
As I must reason. First reflect on this:
Supposest thou that one would rather choose
To reign with fears than sleeping calmest sleep,
His power being equal? I, for one, prize less
The name of king than deeds of kingly power;
And so would all who learn in wisdom's school.
Now without fear I have what I desire,
At thy hand given. Did I rule, myself,
I might do much unwillingly. Why, then,
Should sovereignty exert a softer charm
Than power and might unchequered by a care?
I am not yet so cheated by myself
As to desire aught else but honest gain.
Now all goes well, now every one salutes,
Now they who seek thy favour court my smiles,
For on this hinge does all their fortune turn.
Why, then, should I leave this to hunt for that?
My mind, retaining reason, ne'er could act
The villain's part. I was not born to love
Such thoughts myself, nor bear with those that do.
And as a proof of this, go thou thyself,
And ask at Pytho whether I brought back,
In very deed, the oracles I heard.
And if thou find me plotting with the seer,
In common concert, not by one decree,
But two, thine own and mine, proclaim my death.
But charge me not with crime on shadowy proof;
For neither is it just, in random thought,
The bad to count as good, nor good as bad;

For to thrust out a friend of noble heart,
Is like the parting with the life we love.
And this in time thou'lt know, for time alone
Makes manifest the righteous. Of the vile
Thou mayst detect the vileness in a day.

CHORUS.
To one who fears to fall, he speaketh well;
O king, swift counsels are not always safe.

OEDIP.
But when a man is swift in wily schemes,
Swift must I be to baffle plot with plot;
And if I stand and wait, he wins the day,
And all my life is found one great mistake.

CREON.
What seek'st thou, then? to drive me from the land?

OEDIP.
Not so. I seek not banishment, but death.

CREON.
When thou show'st first what grudge I bear to thee?

OEDIP.
And say'st thou this defying, yielding not?

CREON.
I see thy judgment fails.

OEDIP.
I hold mine own.

CREON.

> Mine has an equal claim.

OEDIP.

> Thou villain born!

CREON.

> And if thy mind is darkened...?

OEDIP.

> Still obey!

CREON.

> Not to a tyrant ruler.

OEDIP.

> O my country!

CREON.

> I, too, can claim that country. 'Tis not thine!

CHORUS.

> Cease, O my princes! In good time I see
> Jocasta coming hither from the house;
> And it were well with her to hush this strife.

[*Enter* JOCASTA]

JOC.

> Why, O ye wretched ones, this strife of tongues
> Raise ye in your unwisdom, nor are shamed,
> Our country suffering, private griefs to stir?
> Come thou within. And thou, O Creon, go,
> Nor bring a trifling sore to mischief great!

CREON.

> My sister! Oedipus, thy husband, claims
> The right to wrong me, giving choice of ills,
> Or to be exiled from my home, or die.

OEDIP.

> 'Tis even so, for I have found him, wife,
> Against my life his evil wiles devising.

CREON.

> May I ne'er prosper, but accursed die,
> If I have done the things he says I did!

JOC.

> Oh, by the Gods, believe him, Oedipus!
> Respect his oath, which calls the Gods to hear;
> And reverence me, and these who stand by thee.

CHORUS.

> Hearken, my king! be calmer, I implore!

OEDIP.

> What! wilt thou that I yield?

CHORUS.

> Respect is due
> To one not weak before, who now is strong
> In this his oath.

OEDIP.

> And know'st thou what thou ask'st?

CHORUS.

> I know right well.

OEDIP.

Say on, then, what thou wilt.

CHORUS.

Hurl not to shame, on grounds of mere mistrust,
The friend on whom his own curse still must hang.

OEDIP.

Know, then, that, seeking this, thou seek'st, in truth,
To work my death, or else my banishment.

CHORUS.

Nay, by the sun, chief God of all the Gods!
May I, too, die, of God and man accursed,
If I wish aught like this! But on my soul,
Our wasting land dwells heavily; ills on ills
Still coming, and your strife embittering all.

OEDIP.

Let him depart, then, even though I die,
Or from my country wander forth in shame:
Thy face, not his, I view with pitying eye;
For him, where'er he be, is naught but hate.

CREON.

Thou'rt loath to yield, 'twould seem, and wilt be vexed
When this thy wrath is over: moods like thine
Are fitly to themselves most hard to bear.

OEDIP.

Wilt thou not go, and leave me?

CREON.
I will go,
By thee misjudged, but known as just by these.
[*Exit.*]

CHORUS.
Why, lady, art thou slow to lead him in?

JOC.
I fain would learn how this sad chance arose.

CHORUS.
Blind hasty speech there was, and wrong will sting.

JOC.
From both of them?

CHORUS.
Yea, both.

JOC.
And what said each?

CHORUS.
Enough for me, our land laid low in grief,
It seems, to leave the quarrel where it stopped.

OEDIP.
Seest thou, with all thy purposes of good,
Thy shifting and thy soothing, what thou dost?

CHORUS.

> My chief, not once alone I spoke,
> And wild and erring should I be,
> Were I to turn from thee aside,
> Who, when my country rocked in storm,
> Righted her course, and, if thou couldst,
> Wouldst send her speeding now.

JOC.

> Tell me, my king, what cause of fell debate
> Has bred this discord, and provoked thy soul.

OEDIP.

> Thee will I tell, for thee I honour more
> Than these. The cause was Creon and his plots.

JOC.

> Say, then, if clearly thou canst tell the strife.

OEDIP.

> He says that I am Laius' murderer.

JOC.

> Of his own knowledge, or by some one taught?

OEDIP.

> Yon scoundrel seer suborning. For himself,
> He takes good care to free his lips from blame.

JOC.

> Leave now thyself, and all thy thoughts of this,
> And list to me, and learn how little skill
> In arts prophetic mortal man may claim;
> And of this truth I'll give thee proof full clear.
> There came to Laius once an oracle
> (I say not that it came from Phœbus' self,
> But from his servants) that his fate was fixed
> By his son's hand to fall—his own and mine:
> And him, so rumour runs, a robber band
> Of aliens slew, where meet the three great roads.
> Nor did three days succeed the infant's birth,
> Before, by other hands, he cast him forth,
> Maiming his ankles, on a lonely hill.
> Here, then, Apollo failed to make the boy
> His father's murderer; nor did Laius die
> By his son's hand. So fared the oracles;
> Therefore regard them not. Whate'er the God
> Desires to search he will himself declare.

OEDIP. [*trembling*]

> O what a fearful boding! thoughts disturbed
> Thrill through my soul, my queen, at this thy tale.

JOC.

> What means this shuddering, this averted glance?

OEDIP.

> I thought I heard thee say that Laius died,
> Slain in a skirmish where the three roads meet?

JOC.

> So was it said, and still the rumours hold.

OEDIP.

Where was the spot in which this matter passed?

JOC.

They call the country Phocis, and the roads
From Delphi and from Daulia there converge.

OEDIP.

And time? what interval has passed since then?

JOC.

But just before thou camest to possess
And rule this land the tidings were proclaimed.

OEDIP.

Great Zeus! what fate hast thou decreed for me?

JOC.

What thought is this, my Oedipus, of thine?

OEDIP.

Ask me not yet, but tell of Laius' frame,
His build, his features, and his years of life.

JOC.

Tall was he, and the white hairs snowed his head,
And in his face not much unlike to thee.

OEDIP.

Woe, woe is me! so seems it I have plunged
All blindly into curses terrible.

JOC.

What sayest thou? I shudder as I see thee.

OEDIP.

Desponding fear comes o'er me, lest the seer
Has seen indeed. But one thing more I'll ask.

JOC.

I fear to speak, yet what thou ask'st I'll tell.

OEDIP.

Went he in humble guise, or with a troop
Of spearmen, as becomes a man that rules?

JOC.

Five were they altogether, and of them
One was a herald, and one chariot had he.

OEDIP.

Woe! woe! 'tis all too clear. And who was he
That told these tidings to thee, O my queen?

JOC.

A servant who alone escaped with life.

OEDIP.

And does he chance to dwell among us now?

JOC.

Not so; for from the time when he returned,
And found thee bearing sway, and Laius dead,
He, at my hand, a suppliant, implored
This boon, to send him to the distant fields
To feed his flocks, where never glance of his
Might Thebes behold. And so I sent him forth;
For though a slave he might have claimed yet more.

OEDIP.

And could we fetch him quickly back again?

JOC.

That may well be. But why dost thou wish this?

OEDIP.

I fear, O queen, that words best left unsaid
Have passed these lips, and therefore wish to see him.

JOC.

Well, he shall come. But some small claim have I,
O king, to learn what touches thee with woe.

OEDIP.

Thou shalt not fail to learn it, now that I
Have such forebodings reached. To whom should I
More than to thee tell all the passing chance?
I had a father, Polybus of Corinth,
And Merope of Doris was my mother,
And I was held in honour by the rest
Who dwelt there, till this accident befel,
Worthy of wonder, of the heat unworthy
It roused within me. Thus it chanced: A man
At supper, in his cups, with wine o'ertaken,
Reviles me as a spurious changeling boy;
And I, sore vexed, hardly for that day
Restrained myself. And when the morrow came
I went and charged my father and my mother
With what I thus had heard. They heaped reproach
On him who stirred the matter, and I soothed
My soul with what they told me; yet it teased,
Still vexing more and more; and so I went,
Unknown to them, to Pytho, and the God

Sent me forth shamed, unanswered in my quest;
And more he added, dread and dire and dark,
How that the doom of incest lay on me,
Most foul, unnatural; and that I should be
Father of children men would loathe to look on,
And murderer of the father that begot me.
And, hearing this, I cast my wistful looks
To where the stars hang over Corinth's towers,
And fled where nevermore mine eyes might see
The shame of those dire oracles fulfilled;
And as I went I reached the spot where he,
The king, thou tell'st me, met the fatal blow.
And now, O lady, I will tell thee all.
Wending my steps that way where three roads meet,
There met me first a herald, and a man
Like him thou told'st of, riding on his car,
Drawn by young colts. With rough and hasty words
They drove me from the road,—the driver first,
And that old man himself; and then in rage
I struck the driver, who had turned me back.
And when the old man saw it, watching me
As by the chariot side I stood, he struck
My forehead with a double-pointed goad.
But we were more than quits, for in a trice
With this right hand I struck him with my staff,
And he rolled backward from his chariot's seat.
And then I slew them all. And if it chance
That Laius and this stranger are akin,
What man more wretched than this man who speaks,
What man more harassed by the vexing Gods?
He whom none now, or alien, or of Thebes,
May welcome to their house, or speak to him,
But thrust him forth an exile. And 'twas I,
None other, who against myself proclaimed
These curses. And the bed of him that died

I with my hands, by which he fell, defile.
Am I not vile by nature, all unclean?
If I must flee, yet still in flight my doom
Is nevermore to see the friends I love,
Nor tread my country's soil; or else to bear
The guilt of incest, and my father slay,
Yea, Polybus, who reared me from the womb.
Would not a man say right who said that here
Some cruel God was pressing hard on me?
Not that, not that, at least, thou Presence, pure
And awful, of the Gods. May I ne'er look
On such a day as that, but far away
Depart unseen from all the haunts of men
Before such great pollution comes on me.

CHORUS.
Us, too, O king, these things perplex, yet still,
Till thou hast asked the man who then was by,'
Have hope.

OEDIP.
And this indeed is all my hope,
Waiting until that shepherd-slave appear.

JOC.
And when he comes, what meanest thou to ask?

OEDIP.
I'll tell thee. Should he now repeat the tale
Thou told'st to me, it frees me from this guilt.

JOC.
What special word was that thou heard'st from me?

OEDIP.

> Thou said'st he told that robbers slew his lord,
> And should he give their number as the same
> Now as before, it was not I who slew him,
> For one man could not be the same as many.
> But if he speak of one man, all alone,
> Then, all too plain, the deed cleaves fast to me.

JOC.

> But know, the thing was said, and clearly said,
> And now he cannot from his word draw back.
> Not I alone, but the whole city, heard it;
> And should he now retract his former tale,
> Not then, my husband, will he rightly show
> The death of Laius, who, as Loxias told,
> By my son's hand should die; and yet, poor boy,
> He killed him not, but perished long ago.
> So I for one, both now and evermore,
> Will count all oracles as things of naught.

OEDIP.

> Thou reasonest well. Yet send a messenger
> To fetch that peasant. Be not slack in this.

JOC.

> I will make haste to send. But go thou in;
> I would do nothing that displeaseth thee.
> [*Exeunt*.]

STROPHE I

CHORUS.
 O that my fate were fixed
 To live in holy purity of speech,
 Pure in all deeds whose laws stand firm and high,
  In heaven's clear æther born,
 Of whom Olympus only is the sire,
  Whom man's frail flesh begat not,
 Nor ever shall forgetfulness o'erwhelm;
 In them our God is great and grows not old.

ANTISTROPHE I

But pride begets the mood of tyrant power;
Pride filled with many thoughts, yet filled in vain,
 Untimely, ill-advised,
 Scaling the topmost height,
 Falls down the steep abyss,
Down to the pit, where step that profiteth
 It seeks in vain to take.
I cannot ask the Gods to stop midway
The conflict sore that works our country's good;
I cannot cease to call on God for aid.

STROPHE II

But if there be who walketh haughtily,
 In action or in speech,
Whom righteousness herself has ceased to awe,
Who counts the temples of the Gods profane,
 An evil fate be his,
Fit meed for all his boastfulness of heart;
Unless in time to come he gain his gains

All justly, and draws back from godless deeds,
Nor lays rash hand upon the holy things,
    By man inviolable.
If such deeds prosper who will henceforth pray
To guard his soul from passion's fiery darts?
If such as these are held in high repute,
What profit is there of my choral strain?

ANTISTROPHE II

No longer will I go in pilgrim guise,
To yon all holy place, Earth's central shrine,
    Nor unto Abae's temple,
    Nor to far-famed Olympia,
Unless these pointings of a hand divine
In sight of all men stand out clear and true.
But, O thou sovereign ruler! if that name,
O Zeus, belongs to thee, who reign'st o'er all,
Let not this trespass hide itself from thee,
    Or thine undying sway;
    For now they set at naught
    The oracles, half dead,
    That Laius heard of old,
And king Apollo's wonted worship flags,
    And all to wreck is gone
    The homage due to God.

    [*Enter* JOCASTA, *followed by an Attendant*]

JOC.
    Princes of this our land, across my soul
    There comes the thought to go from shrine to shrine
    Of all the Gods, these garlands in my hand,
    And waving incense; for our Oedipus
    Vexes his soul too wildly with his woes,

And speaks not as a man should speak who scans
The present by the experience of the past,
But hangs on every breath that tells of fear.
And since I find that my advice avails not,
To thee, Lyceian King, Apollo, first
I come,—for thou art nearest,—suppliant
With these devotions, trusting thou wilt work
Some way of healing for us, free from guilt;
For now we shudder, all of us, seeing him,
The good ship's pilot, panic-struck and lost.

[*Enter* MESSENGER]

MESS.

May I inquire of you, O strangers, where
To find the house of Oedipus the king,
And, above all, where he is, if ye know?

CHORUS.

This is the house, and he, good sir, within,
And this his wife, and mother of his children.

MESS.

Good fortune be with her and all her kin,
Being, as she is, his true and honoured wife.

JOC.

Like fortune be with thee, my friend. Thy speech,
So kind, deserves no less. But tell me why
Thou comest, what thou hast to ask or tell.

MESS.

Good news to thee, and to thy husband, lady.

JOC.

What is it, then? and who has sent thee here?

MESS.

I come from Corinth, and the news I'll tell
May give thee joy. Why not? Yet thou mayst grieve.

JOC.

What is the news that has this twofold power?

MESS.

The citizens that on these Isthmus dwell
Will make him sovereign. So the rumour ran.

JOC.

What then? Is aged Polybus no more?

MESS.

E'en so. Death holds him in the stately tomb.

JOC.

What say'st thou? Polybus, thy king, is dead?

MESS.

If I speak false, I have no wish to live!

JOC.

Go, maiden, at thy topmost speed, and tell
Thy master this. Now, oracles of Gods,
Where are ye now? Long since my Oedipus
Fled, fearing lest his hand should slay the man;
And now he dies by fate, and not by him.

[*Enter* OEDIPUS]

OEDIP.

Mine own Jocasta, why, O dearest one,
Why hast thou sent to fetch me from the house?

JOC.

List this man's tale, and when thou hearest, see
The woeful plight of those dread oracles.

OEDIP.

Who, then, is this, and what has he to tell?

JOC.

He comes from Corinth, and he brings thee word
That Polybus, thy father, lives no more.

OEDIP.

What say'st thou, friend? Tell me thy tale thyself.

MESS.

If I must needs report the story clear,
Know well that he has gone the way of death.

OEDIP.

Was it by plot, or chance of natural death?

MESS.

An old man's frame a little stroke lays low!

OEDIP.

He suffered, then, it seems, from some disease?

MESS.

E'en so, and many a weary month he passed.

OEDIP.

Ha! ha! Why now, my queen, should we regard
The Pythian hearth oracular, or birds
In mid-air crying? By their auguries,
I was to slay my father. And he dies,
And the grave hides him; and I find myself
Handling no sword; unless for love of me
He pined away, and so I caused his death.
So Polybus is gone, and with him lie,
In Hades whelmed, those worthless oracles.

JOC.

Did I not tell thee this long time ago?

OEDIP.

Thou didst, but I was led away by fears.

JOC.

Dismiss them, then, for ever from thy thoughts!

OEDIP.

And yet that "incest"; must I not fear that?

JOC.

Why should we fear, when chance rules everything,
And foresight of the future there is none;
'Tis best to live at random, as one can.
But thou, fear not that marriage with thy mother:
Such things men oft have dreams of; but who cares
The least about them lives the happiest.

OEDIP.

Right well thou speakest all things, save that she
Still lives that bore me, and I can but fear,
Seeing that she lives, although thou speakest well.

JOC.

    And yet thy father's grave's a spot of light.

OEDIP.

    'Tis so: yet while she liveth there is fear.

MESS.

    Who is this woman about whom ye fear?

OEDIP.

    'Tis Merope, old sir, who lived with Polybus.

MESS.

    And what leads you to think of her with fear?

OEDIP.

    A fearful oracle, my friend, from God.

MESS.

    Canst tell it; or must others ask in vain?

OEDIP.

    Most readily; for Loxias said of old
    The doom of incest lay on me, and I
    With mine own hands should spill my father's blood.
    And therefore Corinth long ago I left,
    And journeyed far, right prosperously I own;—
    And yet 'tis sweet to see a parent's face.

MESS.

    And did this fear thy steps to exile lead?

OEDIP. I did not wish to take my father's life.

MESS.

    Why, the, O king, did I who came with good
    Not free thee from this fear that haunts thy soul?

OEDIP.

    For this, I own, I owe thee worthy thanks.

MESS.

    For this, I own, I chiefly came to thee;
    That I on thy return may prosper well.

OEDIP.

    But I return not while a parent lives.

MESS.

    'Tis clear, my son, thou know'st not what thou dost.

OEDIP.

    What is't? By all the Gods, old man, speak out.

MESS.

    If 'tis for them thou fearest to return…

OEDIP.

    I fear lest Phœbus prove himself too true.

MESS.

    Is it lest thou shouldst stain thy soul through them?

OEDIP.

    This selfsame fear, old man, for ever haunts me.

MESS.

    And know'st thou not there is no cause for fear?

OEDIP.

Is there no cause if I was born their son?

MESS.

None is there. Polybus is naught to thee.

OEDIP.

What say'st thou? Did not Polybus beget me?

MESS.

No more than he thou speak'st to; just as much.

OEDIP.

How could a father's claim become as naught?

MESS.

Well, neither he begat thee nor did I.

OEDIP.

Why, then, did he acknowledge me as his?

MESS.

He at my hands received thee as a gift.

OEDIP.

And could he love another's child so much?

MESS.

Yes; for this former childlessness wrought on him.

OEDIP.

And gav'st thou me as buying or as finding?

MESS.

I found thee in Kithæron's shrub-grown hollow.

OEDIP.
    And for what cause didst travel thitherwards?

MESS.
    I had the charge to tend the mountain flocks.

OEDIP.
    Was thou a shepherd born, or seeking hire?

MESS.
    At any rate, my son, I saved thee then.

OEDIP.
    What evil, plight, then, didst thou find me in?

MESS.
    The sinews of thy feet would tell that tale.

OEDIP.
    Ah, me! why speak'st thou of that ancient wrong?

MESS.
    I freed thee when thy insteps both were pierced.

OEDIP.
    A foul disgrace I had in swaddling clothes.

MESS.
    Thus from his chance there came the name thou bearest.

OEDIP. [*starting*]
    Who gave the name, my father or my mother;
    In heaven's name tell me?

MESS.

> This I do not know;
> Who gave thee to me better knows than I.

OEDIP.

> Didst thou, then, take me from another's hand,
> Not finding me thyself?

MESS.

> Not I, indeed;
> Another shepherd made a gift of thee.

OEDIP.

> Who was he? know'st thou where to find him out?

MESS.

> They called him one of those that Laius owned.

OEDIP.

> Mean's thou the former sovereign of this land?

MESS.

> E'en so. He fed the flocks of him thou nam'st.

OEDIP.

> And is he living still that I might see him?

MESS.

> You, his own countrymen, should know that best.

OEDIP.

> Is there of you who stand and listen here
> One who has known the shepherd that he tells of,
> Or seeing him upon the hills or here?
> If so, declare it; 'tis full time to speak!

CHORUS.

    I think that this is he whom from the hills
    But now thou soughtest. But Jocasta here
    Could tell thee this with surer word than I.

OEDIP.

    Knowest thou, my queen, the man whom late we sent
    To fetch; and him of whom this stranger speaks?

JOC. [*with forced calmness*]

    Whom did he speak of? Care not thou for it,
    But wish his words may be but idle tales.

OEDIP.

    I cannot fail, once getting on the scent,
    To track at last the secret of my birth.

JOC.

    Ah, by the Gods, if that thou valuest life
    Inquire no further. Let my woe suffice.

OEDIP.

    Take heart; though I should turn out thrice a slave,
    Born of a thrice vile mother, thou art still
    Free from all stain.

    JOC.

    Yet, I implore thee, pause!
    Yield to my counsels, do not do this deed.

OEDIP.

    I may not yield, and fail to search it out.

JOC.

> And yet good counsels give I, for thy good.

OEDIP.

> This "for my good" has been my life's long plague.

JOC.

> Who thou art, hapless, mayst thou never know!

OEDIP.

> Will some one bring that shepherd to me here?
> Leave her to glory in her high descent.

JOC.

> Woe! woe! ill-fated one! my last word this,
> This only, and no more for evermore.
> [*Rushes out.*]

CHORUS.

> Why has thy queen, O Oedipus, gone forth
> In her wild sorrow rushing. Much I fear
> Lest from such silence evil deeds burst out.

OEDIP.

> Burst out what will, I seek to know my birth,
> Low though it be, and she perhaps is shamed
> (For, like a woman, she is proud of heart)
> At thoughts of my low birth; but I, who count
> Myself the child of Fortune, fear no shame.
> My mother she, and she has prospered me.
> And so the months that span my life have made me
> Both high and low; but whatsoe'er I be,
> Such as I am I am, and needs must on
> To fathom all the secret of my birth.

STROPHE

CHORUS.
>   If the seer's gift be mine,
>   Or skill in counsel wise,
>   Thou, O Kithæron, when the morrow comes,
>   Our full-moon festival,
>   Shalt fail not to resound
>   The voice that greets thee, fellow-citizen,
>   Parent and nurse of Oedipus;
>   And we will on thee weave our choral dance,
>   As bringing to our princes glad good news.
>   Hail, hail! O Phœbus, smile on this our prayer.

ANTISTROPHE

>   Who was it, child, that bore thee?
>   Blest daughter of the ever-living Ones,
>   Or meeting in the ties of love with Pan,
>   Who wanders o'er the hills,
>   Or with thee, Loxias, for to thee are dear
>   All the high lawns where roam the pasturing flocks;
>   Or was it he who rules Kyllene's height;
>   Or did the Bacchic God,
>   Upon the mountain's peak,
>   Receive thee as the gift of some fair nymph
>   Of Helicon's fair band,
>   With whom he sports and wantons evermore?

OEDIP.

If I must needs conjecture, who as yet
Ne'er met the man, I think I see the shepherd,
Whom this long while we sought for. With the years
His age fits well. And now I see, besides,
My servants bring him. Thou perchance canst say
From former knowledge yet more certainly.

CHORUS.

I know him well, O king! For this man stood,
If any, known as Laius' faithful slave.

[*Enter* Shepherd]

OEDIP.

Thee first I ask, Corinthian stranger, say,
Is this the man?

MESS.

The very man thou seek'st.

OEDIP.

Ho, there, old man. Come hither, look on me,
And tell me all. Did Laius own thee once?

SHEP.

Not as a slave from market, but home-reared.

OEDIP.

What was thy work, or what thy mode of life?

SHEP.

Near all my life I followed with the flock.

OEDIP.
And in what regions didst thou chiefly dwell?

SHEP.
Now 'twas Kithæron, now on neighbouring fields.

OEDIP.
Know'st thou this man? Didst ever see him there?

SHEP.
What did he do? Of what man speakest thou?

OEDIP.
This man now present. Did ye ever meet?

SHEP.
My memory fails when taxed thus suddenly.

MESS.
No wonder that, my lord. But I'll remind him
Right well of things forgotten. Well I know
He'll call to mind when on Kithæron's fields,
He with a double flock, and I with one,
I was his neighbour during three half years,
From springtide on to autumn; and in winter
I drove my flocks to mine own fold, and he
To those of Laius. [*To* SHEPHERD] Is this false or
    true?

SHEP.
Thou tell'st the truth, although long years have passed.

MESS.

    Come, then, say, on. Rememberest thou a boy
    Thou gav'st me once, that I might rear him up
    As mine own child?

SHEP.

    Why askest thou of this?

MESS.

    Here stands he, fellow! that same tiny boy!

SHEP.

    A curse befall thee! Wilt not hold thy tongue?

OEDIP.

    Rebuke him not, old man; thy words need more
    The language of reproaches than do his.

SHEP. .

    Say, good my lord, what fault have I committed?

OEDIP.

    This, that thou tell'st not of the child he asks for.

SHEP.

    Yes, for he speaks in blindness, wasting breath.

OEDIP.

    Thou wilt not speak for favour, but a blow...
    [*Strikes him.*]

SHEP.

    By all the Gods, hurt not my feeble age.

OEDIP.

Will no one bind his hands behind his back?

SHEP.

O man most wretched! what, then, wilt thou learn?

OEDIP.

Gav'st thou this man the boy of whom he asks?

SHEP.

I gave him. Would that day had been my last!

OEDIP.

That doom will soon be thine if thou speak'st wrong.

SHEP.

Nay, much more shall I perish if I speak.

OEDIP.

This fellow, as it seems, would tire us out.

SHEP.

Not so. I said long since I gave it him.

OEDIP.

Whence came it? Was the child thine own or not?

SHEP.

Mine own 'twas not, but some one gave it me,

OEDIP.

Which of our people, or beneath what roof?

SHEP.

Oh, by the Gods, my master, ask no more!

OEDIP.

Thou diest if I question this again.

SHEP.

Some one it was in Laius' household born.

OEDIP. Was it a slave, or some one born to him?

SHEP.

Ah, me! I stand upon the very brink
Where most I dread to speak.

OEDIP.

And I to hear:
And yet I needs must hear it, come what may.

SHEP.

The boy was said to be his son; but she,
Thy queen within, could tell thee best the truth.

OEDIP.

What! was it she who gave it?

SHEP.

Yea, O king!

OEDIP.

And to what end?

SHEP.

To make away with it.

OEDIP.

And dared a mother...?

SHEP.
Evil doom she feared.

OEDIP.
What doom?

SHEP.
'Twas said that he his sire should kill.

OEDIP.
Why, then, didst thou to this old man resign him?

SHEP.
I pitied him, O master, and I thought
That he would bear him to another land,
Whence he himself had come. But him he saved
For direst evil. For if thou be he
Whom this man speaks of, thou art born to ill.

OEDIP.
Woe! woe! woe! woe! all cometh clear at last.
O light, may I ne'er look on thee again,
Who now am seen owing my birth to those
To whom I ought not, and with whom I ought not
In wedlock living, whom I ought not slaying.
[*Exit.*]

STROPHE I

CHORUS.
>Ah, race of mortal men,
>How as a thing of naught
>I count ye, though ye live;
>For who is there of men
>That more of blessing knows
>Than just a little while
>In a vain show to stand,
>And, having stood, to fall?
>With thee before mine eyes,
>Thy destiny, e'en thine,
>Ill-fated Oedipus,
>I can count no man blest.

ANTISTROPHE I

>For thou, with wondrous skill,
>Taking thine aim, didst hit
>Success, in all things prosperous;
>And didst, O Zeus! destroy
>The Virgin with her talons bent,
>And sayings wild and dark;
>And against many deaths
>A tower and strong defence
>Didst for my country rise;
>And therefore dost thou bear the name of king,
>With highest glory crowned,
>Ruling in mighty Thebes.

STROPHE II

And now, who lives than thou more miserable?
Who equals thee in wild woes manifold,
    In shifting turns of life?
    Ah, noble one, our Oedipus!
    For whom the selfsame port
    Sufficed for sire and son,
    In wedlock's haven met:
Ah how, ah how, thou wretched one, so long
    Could that incestuous bed
    Receive thee, and be dumb?

ANTISTROPHE II

Time, who sees all things, he hath found thee out,
Against thy will, and long ago condemned
    The wedlock none may wed,
    Begetter and begotten
    In strange confusion joined.
    Ah, child of Laius! ah!
Would that I ne'er had looked upon thy face!
    For I mourn sore exceedingly,
    From lips with wailing full.
In simplest truth, by thee I rose from death,
By thee I close mine eyes in deadly sleep.

[*Enter Second Messenger*]

SEC. MESS.

Ye chieftains, honoured most in this our land,
For all the deeds ye hear of, all ye see,
How great a wailing will ye raise, if still
Ye truly love the house of Labdacus;
For sure I think that neither Ister's stream
Nor Phasis' floods could purify this house,
Such horrors does it hold. But all too soon,
Will we or will we not, they'll come to light.
Self-chosen sorrows ever pain men most.

CHORUS.

The ills we knew before lacked nothing meet
For plaint and moaning. Now, what add'st thou more?

SEC. MESS.

Quickest for me to speak, and thee to learn;
Our godlike queen Jocasta—she is dead.

CHORUS.

Ah, crushed with many sorrows! How and why?

SEC. MESS.

Herself she slew. The worst of all that passed
I must pass o'er, for none were there to see.
Yet, far as memory suffers me to speak,
That sorrow-stricken woman's end I'll tell;
How, yielding to her passion, on she passed
Within the porch, made straightway for the couch,
Her bridal bed, with both hands tore her hair,
And as she entered, dashing through the doors,
Calls on her Laius, dead long years ago,
Remembering all that birth of long ago,
Which brought him death, and left to her who bore,

With his own son a hateful motherhood.
And o'er her bed she wailed, where she had borne
Spouse to her spouse, and children to her child;
And how she perished after this I know not;
For Oedipus struck in with woeful cry,
And we no longer looked upon her fate,
But gazed on him as to and fro he rushed,
For so he comes, and asks us for a sword,
Wherewith to smite the wife that wife was none,
The bosom stained by those accursed births,
Himself, his children—so, as thus he raves,
Some spirit shows her to him (none of us
Who stood hard by had done so): with a shout
Most terrible, as some one led him on,
Through the two gates he leapt, and from the hasp
He slid the hollow bolt, and falls within;
And there we saw his wife had hung herself,
By twisted cords suspended. When her form
He saw, poor wretch! with one wild, fearful cry,
The twisted rope he loosens, and she fell,
Ill-starred one, on the ground. Then came a sight
Most fearful. Tearing from her robe the clasps,
All chased with gold, with which she decked herself,
He with them struck the pupils of his eyes,
Such words as these exclaiming: "They should see
No more the ills he suffered or had done;
But in the dark should look, in time to come,
On those they ought not, not know whom they would."
With such like wails, not once or twice alone,
Raising the lids, he tore his eyes, and they,
All bleeding, stained his cheek, nor ceased to pour
Thick clots of gore, but still the purple shower
Fell fast and full, a very rain of blood.
Such were the ills that fell on both of them,
Not on one only, wife and husband both.

His former fortune, which he held of old,
Was rightly honoured; but for this day's doom
Wailing and woe, and death and shame, all forms
That man can name of evil, none have failed.

CHORUS.

And hath the wretched man a pause of ill?

SEC. MESS.

He calls to us to ope the gates, and show
To all in Thebes his father's murderer,
His mother's... Foul and fearful were the words
He spoke. I dare not speak them. Then he said
That he would cast himself adrift, nor stay
At home accursèd, as himself had cursed.
Some stay he surely needs, or guiding hand,
For greater is the ill than he can bear,
And this he soon will show thee, for the bolts
Of the two gates are opening, and thou'lt see
A sight to touch e'en hatred's self with pity.

[*The doors of the Palace are thrown open,
and* OEDIPUS *is seen within.*]

CHORUS.

Oh, fearful, piteous sight!
Most fearful of all woes
I hitherto have known! What madness strange
Has come on thee, thou wretched one?
What power with one fell swoop,
Ills heaping upon ills,
Each greater than the last,
Has marked thee for its prey?
Woe! woe! thou doomed one, wishing much to ask,
And much to learn, and much to gaze into,

I cannot look on thee,
So horrible the sight!

OEDIP.
Ah, woe! ah, woe! ah, woe!
Woe for my misery!
Where am I wand'ring in my utter woe?
Where floats my voice in air?
Dread power, where leadest thou?

CHORUS.
To doom of dread nor sight nor speech may bear.

OEDIP.
O cloud of darkest guilt
That onwards sweeps with dread ineffable,
Resistless, borne along by evil blast,
Woe, woe, and woe again!
How through my soul there darts the sting of pain,
The memory of my crimes.

CHORUS.
And who can wonder that in such dire woes
Thou mournest doubly, bearing twofold ills?

OEDIP.
Ah, friend,
Thou only keepest by me, faithful found,
Nor dost the blind one slight.
Woe, woe,
For thou escap'st me not, I know thee well;
Though all is dark, I still can hear thy voice.

CHORUS.

O man of fearful deeds, how couldst thou bear
Thine eyes to outrage? What power stirred thee to it?

OEDIP.

Apollo! oh, my friends, the God, Apollo!
Who worketh all my woes—yes, all my woes.
No human hand but mine has done this deed.
What need for me to see,
When nothing's left that's sweet to look upon?

CHORUS.

Too truly dost thou speak the thing that is.

OEDIP.

Yea, what remains to see,
Or what to love, or hear,
With any touch of joy?
Lead me away, my friends, with utmost speed,
Lead me away, the foul polluted one,
Of all men most accursed,
Most hateful to the Gods.

CHORUS.

Ah, wretched one, alike in soul and doom,
Would that my eyes had never known thy face!

OEDIP.

Ill fate be his who loosed the fetters sharp,
That ate into my flesh,
And freed me from the doom of death,
And saved me—thankless boon!
Ah! had I died but then,
Nor to my friends nor me had been such woe.

CHORUS.
    That I, too, vainly wish!

OEDIP.
       Yes; then I had not been
       My father's murderer:
    Nor had men pointed to me as the man
       Wedded with her who bore him.
    But now all god-deserted, born in sins,
    In incest joined with her who gave me birth;
    Yea, if there be an evil worse than all,
       It falls on Oedipus!

CHORUS.
    I may not call thy acts or counsels good,
    For better wert thou dead than living blind.

OEDIP.
    Persuade me not, nor counsel give to show
    That what I did was not the best to do.
    I know not how, on entering Hades dark,
    To look for my own father or my mother,
    Crimes worse than deadly done against them both.
    And though my children's face was sweet to see
    With their growth growing, yet these eyes no more
    That sight shall see, nor citadel, nor tower,
    Nor sacred shrines of Gods whence I, who stood
    Most honoured one in Thebes, myself have banished,
    Commanding all to thrust the godless forth,
    Him whom the Gods do show accursed, the stock
    Of Laius old. And could I dare to look,
    Such dire pollution fixing on myself,
    And meet them face to face? Not so, not so.
    Yea, if I could but stop the stream of sound,

And dam mine ears against it, I would do it,
Closing each wretched sense that I might live
Both blind, and hearing nothing, Sweet 'twould be
To keep the soul beyond the reach of ills.
Why, O Kithæron, didst thou shelter me,
Nor kill me out of hand? I had not shown,
In that case, all men whence I drew my birth.
O Polybus, and Corinth, and the home
I thought was mine, how strange a growth ye reared,
All fair outside, all rotten at the core;
For vile I stand, descended from the vile.
Ye threefold roads and thickets half concealed,
The hedge, the narrow pass where three ways meet,
Which at my hands did drink my father's blood,
Remember ye what deeds I did in you;
What, hither come, I did?—the marriage rites
That gave me birth, and then, commingling all,
In horrible confusion, showed in one
A father, brother, son, all kindreds mixed,
Mother, and wife, and daughter, hateful names,
All foulest deeds that men have ever done.
But, since, where deeds are evil, speech is wrong,
With utmost speed, by all the Gods, or hide,
Or take my life, or cast me in the sea,
Where nevermore your eyes may look on me.
Come, scorn ye not to touch my misery,
But hearken; fear ye not; no soul but I
Can bear the burden of my countless ills.

CHORUS.

The man for what thou need'st is come in time,
Creon, to counsel and to act, for now
He in thy place is left our only guide.

OEDIP.

Ah, me! what language shall I hold to him,
What trust at his hands claim? In all the past
I showed myself to him most vile and base.

[*Enter* CREON]

CREON.

I have not come, O Oedipus, to scorn,
Nor to reproach thee for thy former crimes;
But ye, if ye have lost your sense of shame
For mortal men, yet reverence the light
Of him, our King, the Sun-God, source of life,
Nor sight so foul expose unveiled to view,
Which neither earth, nor shower from heaven nor light,
Can see and welcome. But with utmost speed
Convey him in; for nearest kin alone
Can meetly see and hear their kindred's ills.

OEDIP.

Oh, by the Gods! since thou, beyond my hopes,
Dost come all noble unto me all base,
In one thing hearken. For thy good I ask.

CREON.

And what request seek'st thou so wistfully?

OEDIP.

Cast me with all thy speed from out this land,
Where nevermore a man may look on me!

CREON.

Be sure I would have done so, but I wished
To learn what now the God will bid us do.

OEDIP.

The oracle was surely clear enough
That I, the parricide, the pest, should die.

CREON.

So ran the words. But in our present need
'Tis better to learn surely what to do.

OEDIP.

And will ye ask for one so vile as I?

CREON.

Yea, now thou, too, wouldst trust the voice of God.

OEDIP.

And this I charge thee, yea, and supplicate,
For her within, provide what tomb thou wilt,
For for thine own most meetly thou wilt care;
But never let this city of my fathers
Be sentenced to receive me as its guest;
But suffer me on yon lone hills to dwell,
Where stands Kithæron, chosen as my tomb
While still I lived, by mother and by sire,
That I may die by those who sought to kill.
And yet this much I know, that no disease,
Nor aught else could have killed me; ne'er from death
Had I been saved but for this destined doom.
But for our fate, whatever comes may come:
And for my boys, O Creon, lay no charge
Of them upon me. They are grown, nor need,
Where'er they be, feel lack of means to live.
But for my two poor girls, all desolate,
To whom their table never brought a meal
Without my presence, but whate'er I touched

They still partook of with me; these I care for.
Yea, let me touch them with my hands, and weep
To them my sorrows. Grant it, O my prince,
    O born of noble nature!
Could I but touch them with my hands, I feel
Still I should have them mine, as when I saw.

[*Enter* ANTIGONE *and* ISMENE]

    What say I? What is this?
Do I not hear, ye Gods, their dear, loved tones,
Broken with sobs, and Creon, pitying me,
Hath sent the dearest of my children to me?
    Is it not so?

CREON.

It is so. I am he who gives thee this,
Knowing the joy thou hadst in them of old.

OEDIP.

Good luck have thou! And may the powers on high
Guard thy path better than they guarded mine!
Where are ye, O my children? Come, oh, come
To these your brother's hands, which but now tore
Your father's eyes, that once were bright to see,
Who, O my children, blind and knowing naught,
Became your father—how, I may not tell.
I weep for you, though sight is mine no more,
Picturing in mind the sad and dreary life
Which waits you in the world in years to come;
For to what friendly gatherings will ye go,
Or festive joys, from whence, for stately show
Once yours, ye shall not home return in tears?
And when ye come to marriageable age,
Who is there, O my children, rash enough

To make his own the shame that then will fall
On those who bore me, and on you as well?
What evil fails us here? Your father killed
His father, and was wed in incest foul
With her who bore him, and ye owe your birth
To her who gave him his. Such shame as this
Will men lay on you, and who then will dare
To make you his in marriage? None, not one,
My children! but ye needs must waste away,
Unwedded, childless, Thou, Menœkeus' son,
Since thou alone art left a father to them
(For we, their parents, perish utterly),
Suffer them not to wander husbandless,
Nor let thy kindred beg their daily bread;
But look on them with pity, seeing them
At their age, but for thee, deprived of all.
O noble soul, I pray thee, touch my hand
In token of consent. And ye, my girls,
Had ye the minds to hearken I would fain
Give ye much counsel. As it is, pray for me
To live where'er is meet; and for yourselves
A brighter life than his ye call your sire.

CREON.
    Enough of tears and words. Go thou within.

OEDIP.
    I needs must yield, however, hard it be.

CREON.
    In their right season all things prosper best.

OEDIP.
    Know'st thou my wish?

CREON.
Speak and I then shall hear.

OEDIP.
That thou shouldst send me far away from home.

CREON.
Thou askest what the Gods alone can give.

OEDIP.
And yet I go most hated of the Gods.

CREON.
And therefore it may chance thou gain'st thy wish.

OEDIP.
And dost thou promise, then, to grant it me?

CREON.
I am not wont to utter idle words.

OEDIP.
Lead me, then, hence.

CREON.
Go thou, but leave the girls.

OEDIP.
Ah, take them not from me!

CREON.
Thou must not think
To have thy way in all things all thy life.
Thou hadst it once, yet went it ill with thee.

CHORUS.

Ye men of Thebes, behold this Oedipus,
Who knew the famous riddle and was noblest,
Who envied no one's fortune and success.
And, lo,! in what a sea of direst woe
He now is plunged. From hence the lesson draw,
To reckon no man happy till ye see
The closing day; until he pass the bourn
Which severs life from death, unscathed by woe.

THE END

CPSIA information can be obtained
at www.ICGtesting.com
Printed in the USA
LVOW11s0105281017
554097LV00001B/8/P